Crabs

Jennifer Howse

www.av2books.com

AV² provides enriched content that supplements and complements this book. Weigl's AV² books strive to create inspired learning and engage young minds in a total learning experience.

Your AV² Media Enhanced books come alive with...

Audio
Listen to sections of the book read aloud.

Key Words
Study vocabulary, and complete a matching word activity.

Video
Watch informative video clips.

Quizzes
Test your knowledge.

Embedded Weblinks
Gain additional information for research.

Slide Show
View images and captions, and prepare a presentation.

Try This!
Complete activities and hands-on experiments.

... and much, much more!

Go to **www.av2books.com**, and enter this book's unique code.

BOOK CODE

C 3 4 9 4 3 0

AV² by Weigl brings you media enhanced books that support active learning.

Published by AV² by Weigl
350 5th Avenue, 59th Floor New York, NY 10118
Website: www.av2books.com   www.weigl.com

Library of Congress Cataloging-in-Publication Data

Howse, Jennifer.
  Crabs / Jennifer Howse.
    p. cm. -- (Ocean Life)
Includes index.
  ISBN 978-1-61690-690-0 (hardcover : alk. paper) -- ISBN 978-1-61690-694-8 (softcover : alk. paper)
  1. Crabs--Juvenile literature. I. Title.
  QL444.M33H685 2012
  595.3'86--dc22

                        2010050416

Printed in the United States of America in North Mankato, Minnesota
1 2 3 4 5 6 7 8 9 0 15 14 13 12 11

052011
WEP37500

Project Coordinator: Jordan McGill
Art Director: Terry Paulhus

Weigl acknowledges Getty Images, Dreamstime, iStockphoto, and Peter Arnold as image suppliers for this title.

CONTENTS

2   AV² Code

4   What is a Crab?

7   Crab Size

8   Baby Crabs

10 Crab Shell

13 Eye Stalks

15 Crab Cuisine

16 Best of Friends

18 Can You Spot the Crab?

21 Crab Safety

22 Crab Hide and Seek

23 Glossary/Index

24 Log on to
    www.av2books.com

What is a Crab?

Have you ever seen a sea animal that wears its bones on the outside of its body? It may have been a crab. A crab is a kind of **shellfish**. Crabs have thick shells and claws.

There are more than 4,500 different kinds of crab. Crabs live on land and in water.

Crabs have eight legs and two claws. They often walk sideways.

5

Crab Size

Did you know the smallest crab is the size of a large pea? The pea crab is only 0.5 inches (1.27 centimeters) wide. The largest crab is the Japanese spider crab. It can grow up to 12 feet (9 meters) wide.

Japanese spider crabs can live as long as 100 years.

Baby Crabs

How different did you look when you were a baby? A baby crab changes from egg to **larva**. Early in life, crabs have tiny hairs that trap food. They float around in the ocean as they grow. Crabs soon grow so heavy that they sink to the ocean floor. There, a shell begins to form over their soft body.

9

Crab Shell

Have you ever outgrown your clothes? Crabs outgrow their shells. Inside the shell, crabs have a soft body that gets larger over time.

As a crab grows, it becomes too big for its shell. The old shell cracks and falls off. A new shell grows to replace the old one. This happens many times in a crab's life.

Hermit crabs do not have a shell of their own. They find objects to live in and use as a shell.

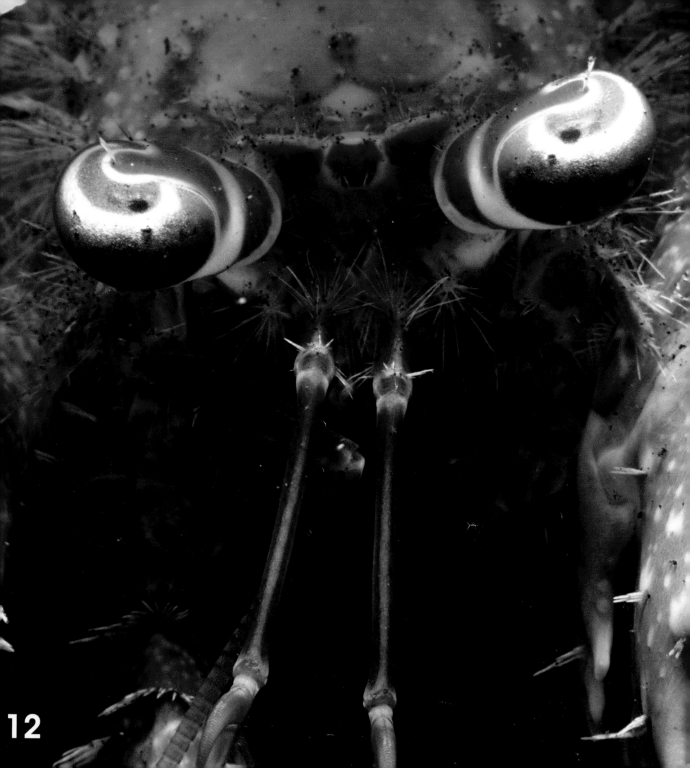

Eye Stalks

Did you know that a crab's eyes stick out from its head? A crab's eyes are located on long, thin tubes called stalks. Crabs can raise or lower the stalks. This helps them see over objects. Crabs can turn their eyes to see in all directions.

The ghost crab was given its name because it looks like Casper the Ghost. Ghost crabs have large, black eyes and white claws.

Crab Cuisine

How do you eat a coconut? Like people, the robber crab breaks coconuts open. The robber crab can smash coconuts with its powerful claws.

Crabs use their claws to grab food. Some of their favorite foods are **algae** and fish. Crabs also like to eat clams and seaweed. Many crabs eat food they find lying around. They do not like to hunt.

Best of Friends

Do you ever wear a watch or necklace? Decorator crabs place other animals and plants, such as sponges and algae, on their shell. These animals and plants hide the crab from octopuses and other **predators.**

The sponge decorator crab puts pieces of sponge on its shell. The sponge keeps growing on the crab. Over time, the crab becomes covered from head to claw.

Can You Spot the Crab?

Have you ever played hide-and-seek? Some crabs are hard to find because they hide from animals that eat them. To hide, these crabs grow a shell that is the same color as their **habitat**.

Other crabs bury themselves in sand. Their eyes poke up above the sand. They can see if a predator or food passes near.

19

Crab Safety

Have you ever held a crab? They can pinch. Crabs do this because they are afraid. Fish, birds, octopuses, sea otters, and some people eat crabs. Sometimes, crabs are not able to hide. They have to use their shells and claws for protection.

Crab Hide and Seek

Supplies

one blue piece of paper, one pink piece of paper, five pieces of onion skin paper, one marker, one glue stick, scissors, and plastic wrap

1. Take the onion skin papers, and draw the shapes of a crab, fish, several plants, and sharks with your felt marker.

2. With the help of an adult, cut out each of these shapes. Put these aside for now. They will be used later to complete an underwater picture.

3. Take your pink piece of construction paper, and lay it flat in front of you. With the felt marker, draw a curvy line through the middle of your paper.

4. Use the scissors to cut carefully along that line.

5. Glue one half of the paper onto the blue paper.

6. Now, take the shapes you cut out earlier. Glue the onion skin paper shapes on and all around the reef. Hide your crab under some plants.

7. Take a piece of plastic wrap, and place it over the entire project. The plastic wrap will protect your creation. It will also make the reef appear as if it is underwater.

8. Ask your friends or family if they can spot your hiding crab.

Glossary

algae: green, slimy plants without roots or leaves that develop in the ocean

habitat: the place where an animal lives in nature

larva: an early stage in a crab's life; it does not have the physical features of an adult crab

predators: animals that hunt other animals for food

shellfish: an animal that lives in water and has a hard covering

Index

claws 4, 15, 16, 21

decorator crab 16

eggs 8
eyes 13, 18

food 15, 18, 23

hermit crab 8, 10

Japanese spider crab 7

pea crab 7
predators 16, 18

shell 4, 8, 10, 16, 18, 21

23

Log on to www.av2books.com

AV² by Weigl brings you media enhanced books that support active learning. Go to www.av2books.com, and enter the special code found on page 2 of this book. You will gain access to enriched and enhanced content that supplements and complements this book. Content includes video, audio, web links, quizzes, a slide show, and activities.

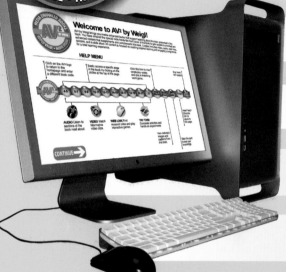

Audio
Listen to sections of the book read aloud.

Video
Watch informative video clips.

Embedded Weblinks
Gain additional information for research.

Try This!
Complete activities and hands-on experiments.

WHAT'S ONLINE?

Try This!

Gain a better understanding of a crab's size with a fun comparison activity.

Identify the benefits of crabs' defensive adaptations.

Complete a fun coloring activity.

Embedded Weblinks

Find more information about crabs.

Check out myths and legends about crabs.

More on a crab's diet and nutrition.

Video

Watch an introductory video to crabs.

Watch a video of a crab in its natural environment.

EXTRA FEATURES

Audio
Listen to sections of the book read aloud.

Key Words
Study vocabulary, and complete a matching word activity.

Slide Show
View images and captions, and prepare a presentation.

Quizzes
Test your knowledge.

AV² was built to bridge the gap between print and digital. We encourage you to tell us what you like and what you want to see in the future. Sign up to be an AV² Ambassador at www.av2books.com/ambassador.